MALDIVES

MALDIVES

NEIL HOOPER

ACKNOWLEDGEMENTS

The Author and Publishers are grateful to the following organizations for permission to reproduce copyright material in this book and for assistance given in its preparation:

Charles Anderson; Susan Buttress; Habib; Hutchison Photo Library; Maldives Government Department of Information and Broadcasting; Department of Linguistic and Historical Research, Malé; Novelty Photo Studio; Phototeknik.

Published by Chelsea House Publishers

First printing

ISBN 0-7910-0160-1

Chelsea House Publishers.
95 Madison Avenue, New York, NY 10016

345 Whitney Avenue, New Haven, CT 05510

5068-B West Chester Pike, Edgemont, PA 19028

Contents

MALDIVES

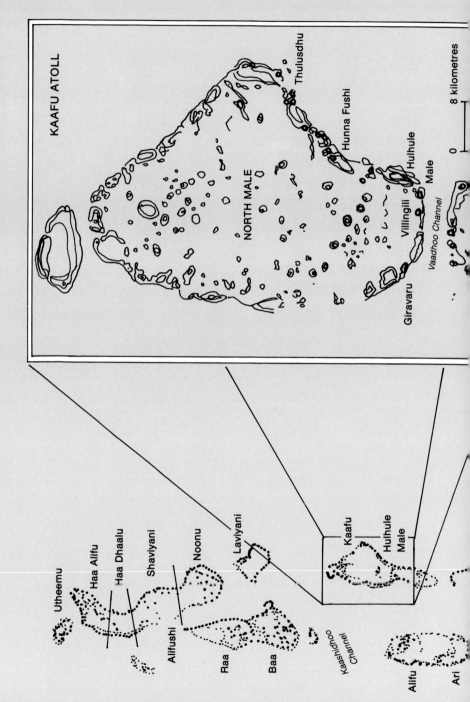

KAAFU ATOLL

Thulusdhu

Hunna Fushi

NORTH MALE

Villingili
Hulhule
Male

Vaadhoo Channel

Giravaru

0   8 kilometres

Utheemu

Haa Alifu

Haa Dhaalu

Shaviyani

Noonu

Laviyani

Alifushi

Raa

Baa

Kaashidhoo Channel

Kaafu
Hulhule
Male

Alifu

Ari

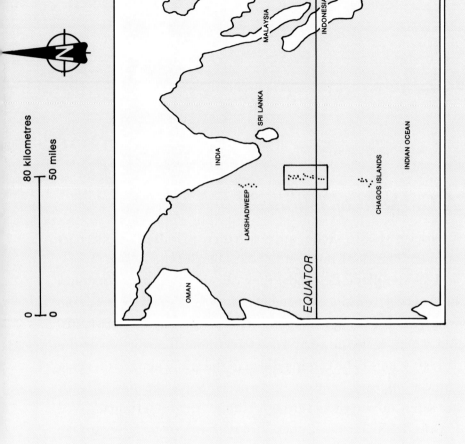

80 kilometres

50 miles

OMAN

INDIA

LAKSHADWEEP

SRI LANKA

MALAYSIA

INDONESIA

CHAGOS ISLANDS

INDIAN OCEAN

EQUATOR

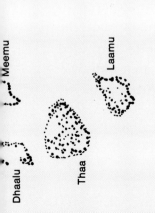

Dhaalu

Meemu

Thaa

Laamu

One and Half Degree Channel

Gaafu Alifu

Huvadu

Gaafu Dhaalu

Equatorial Channel

Fuamulak

Gnyaviyani

Hithadhoo

Addu

Seenu

Gan

A Garland of Islands

Visitors to Maldives today approach these islands in a modern jet airliner. They look down at the dark blue of the Indian Ocean, and, as the plane descends, they can see white breakers on a hidden reef, translucent patches of light blues and greens in the water, then dazzling strips of sand round tiny dark green islands. But where is the airport? Passengers hold their breath as the aircraft seems to be coming down in the sea. Then, suddenly, a runway appears beneath the wheels. Soon the new arrivals are safely on their way through Hulule Airport terminal.

Outside the terminal, there are no buses or taxis; boats take the passengers to the capital or their hotel. For the airport is an island just big enough for a runway and the terminal; Malé, the capital of the Republic of Maldives, is another island—a crowded little island 256 hectares (about square mile) in area with over fifty thousand people living on it. Each tourist resort in the country is an island by itself.

About twelve hundred small coral islands make up this

**An aerial view of Malé, the island capital of the Republic of Maldives —
a garland of islands in the Indian Ocean**

republic in the sea, but only 202 of them are inhabited. About sixty of the uninhabited islands are now tourist resorts, ideal for a "desert island holiday". Thousands of holidaymakers come each year to escape briefly from the stress of modern life, and to enjoy the sun, the near perfect climate, the beaches, and the clear sea with its magic world of coral and tropical fish.

The Maldive Islands are many, but small. The largest is 6.4 kilometres (four miles) long; most are no more than 0.8 kilometres (half a mile) in length. Nobody can decide which sandbank or reef is "the smallest".

The islands stretch for almost 764 kilometres (475 miles) from north to south. They are set out in large rings, called *"atolls"*. *Atoll*

9

Palm trees lining the sandy shore of a coral island. The Republic of Maldives is made up of about twelve hundred small islands

is probably the only word in English that has come from the language of Maldives. This language is called Dhivehi, which just means "the island language" or "Islandish". The people call their country Dhivehi Rajje, that is "The Island Nation". The English name Maldives probably comes from an early description of this chain of islands as "Maladive", a garland of islands. Although many people call the country "The Maldives" or "The Maldive Islands", the official name in English is "Republic of Maldives". That is what is written on its banknotes and postage stamps. Maldives is pronounced *Mawl-divs*. The name of the capital island, Malé, is pronounced *Mal-ey*.

In population (around 182,000) and land area (298 square

kilometres—116 square miles), Maldives is one of the world's smallest independent states, but it has a large sea area 90,000 square kilometres (35,000 sqare miles). The sea provides food for the people of the islands, for it is one of the world's best areas for fishing. The sea is rich in tuna, which is the Maldivian's favourite food, and the traditional basis of the country's economy.

Maldives has always been strategically important, as its islands and reefs form a barrier across the ancient Indian Ocean sea routes. In the days of sail it was difficult to find the few safe channels through the Maldives. Some ships called in for rest and fresh water; others were wrecked on the treacherous reefs. Sailors from these ships must have stayed on to add to the mixture of different peoples living on the islands.

Shoals of tropical fish in the coral reef near Malé

About seven hundred years ago many of these sailors came from the Arab countries west of the Indian Ocean. As a result, the Maldivians adopted the religion which had its origins in Arabia and then spread to many parts of the world—Islam.

The new religion became a strong bond in the island society. Today, it is regarded as a sign of the Maldives' independent culture. The Maldivians have a long history as an independent people, self-contained yet open to outside influence. With modern communications and development, their old way of life is exposed to the world as never before.

Fishermen hauling in their catch. Fishing is the traditional occupation in the islands

Islands from the Sea

The Maldive Islands were formed originally by a chain of underwater mountains stretching southwards from the south-west coast of India to just past the Equator. Millions of years ago, the tops of these mountains reached the surface of the ocean; as they sank, or the water level rose to cover them, perfect conditions were created for coral to grow; warm, clear water, a solid base not too far beneath the surface, and ocean currents bringing in the young coral larvae and food for them.

Larvae is the name given to the young of the coral animal. These larvae are tiny creatures that move with the currents in the sea until they settle on a hard place near the surface. Each one then develops into an adult called a coral polyp. The polyp is small, soft and cylindrical, with a host of thin tentacles on top to catch its food and expel the waste. Each polyp grows for its protection a hard limestone shell, cemented to its base.

The coral polyp can produce more polyps not just by giving birth to young larvae that get carried away by the sea to grow into

13

adults elsewhere, but also by dividing, or "budding", to surround itself with new polyps the same as itself. Each of these new polyps builds its own case beside the parent until a colony of thousands of hard cells is formed. The colonies can grow upwards as well as out; after thousands of years, as new generations of coral polyps build their colonies on the skeletons of the old, a rock-like solid structure develops. This may grow in many different shapes; some of them are really spectacular, depending on the species of coral. What is known as a coral reef is a massive structure of coral that has grown up to the surface of the sea. The coral cannot grow above sea level; a living coral reef will always be covered at high tide.

Coral reefs in the open sea nearly always grow in the shape of a ring. Scientists are not sure exactly why, but it is probably because coral grows best where the open sea brings in plenty of oxygen for the coral to breathe, as well as plankton—tiny plants and animals in the sea—for it to feed on. The coral thus grows out from the centre of the structure; in the centre, the coral dies and gradually settles down below sea level. In this way the typical coral atoll is formed, with a narrow circular reef just breaking the surface of the water and enclosing an area of shallow sea, called a lagoon.

Other creatures contribute to the building of coral islands; an important one is the parrot-fish. This colourful fish feeds off algae—microscopic marine creatures on the coral skeleton. The parrot-fish has such powerful jaws that it can break down the

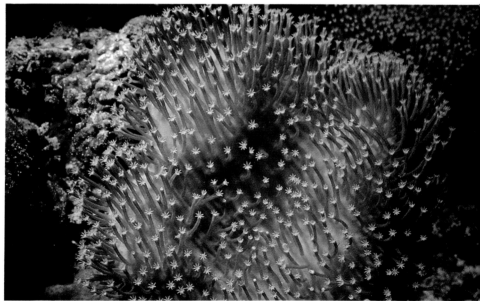

Coral on the sea-bed forming a spectacular underwater "landscape"
which is continually growing and changing

hard limestone skeleton. It is the waste from the parrot-fish's meals that creates the beautiful coral sand which is one of the great assets of the Maldive Islands. It is said that one parrot-fish can easily pass over one tonne of sand per year.

Where this coral sand is built up by the waves on a reef, a sandbank forms. Floating debris builds up there as well, and seeds brought by the wind or by birds can take root. Plants can grow because fresh water is lighter than salt water, and the substance of the developing island can hold fresh rainwater on top of the salt water from the sea. As the vegetation stabilizes the sand, the island grows with more sand and more plants; floating coconuts may be washed up on the beach, and, in time, palm trees grow. The picture of the typical tropical island is complete; a glistening white beach surrounding an area of low bushes, with the crowns of tall palm trees waving above.

Around the island develops another ring of coral, which protects the island from erosion by storm waves, and provides a natural harbour and a shallow sandy lagoon.

None of the islands can grow too large, or the coral will start subsiding in the centre; some of the larger islands have a pool of water in the middle. Most of the larger Maldivian islands are also very narrow, forming part of a large circular chain of coral reef and island. This ring of reefs and islands can stretch up to forty by thirty kilometres (twenty-five by eighteen miles) and enclose a huge lagoon with its own islands and coral rings growing within it. Each of the large systems made up of a ring of coral reef, lagoon and islands is called an atoll.

16

A typical coral island—a glistening white beach surrounding an area of low bushes and palm trees

The chain of atolls of which Maldives forms a part starts near the Indian coast with the Laccadives, (now called the Lakshadweep Islands) which are part of India. South across a 209-kilometre (130-mile) channel, begin the Maldives. From there about twenty-six Maldivian atolls stretch in a chain down to just south of the Equator. Then there are eight hundred kilometres (five hundred miles) of ocean until the system reappears again in the Chagos Islands.

The Maldives chain of atolls is not entirely regular. In the north, the large atolls are long and irregular; they are not well protected from the storms that are common in that region. Southwards from there, the atolls form two lines, split by Kaashidhoo Channel north of Malé atoll. To the south, the lines

17

come together in Thaa and Laam atolls, so that the whole system resembles a giant atoll itself, or the garland that gave Maldives its name.

Then there is a channel of open sea before the southern atolls are reached. First the huge Huvadu atoll, the largest in the world; then, across the Equator in the middle of the wide and turbulent Equatorial Channel, is the island of Fuamulak. This island is one of the most fertile in the Maldives, but it is outside any atoll system. It is surrounded by a protective reef, and has a lake in the centre. Perhaps most of the atolls were like that thousands of years ago, before they expanded and the sea flowed into their sunken centres. Finally, furthest to the south, lies the small but fertile atoll called Addu.

The Island Environment

Because the Maldive chain of islands crosses the Equator, the weather is generally hot and sunny; but the sea winds keep the temperature down and bring quite a lot of rain. Tropical winds blow in a fairly fixed pattern according to the seasons; from May to October the wind is from the south-west, blowing from the coast of Africa across the Indian Ocean up towards the Himalayas. This south-west monsoon, as it is called, brings a few storms and showers of rain. From November to April the north-east monsoon, blowing in the opposite direction, brings some rain at first. Later it settles into long weeks of sunshine. The average annual rainfall is around 1,680 millimetres (70 inches) and the temperature does not vary much from 30 degrees Celsius (86 degrees Fahrenheit).

The vegetation is typical of tropical regions with the coconut palm prominent. Other trees, such as mango, screw pine and banyan are common. The sandy soil and ever-present salt restricts the plants that can flourish in these islands, but the

A giant watermelon ripening in the tropical sun

visitor can still see a few flowering shrubs including the Beach Naupaka with its flower that looks like half a flower, and a variety of night-flowering jasmine. Many people's favourite is the hibiscus tree. In the morning it bears bell-shaped yellow flowers; these darken to deep orange during the afternoon and then fall. Strangely enough, as they lie in the sand under the tree, they all seem to point in the same direction.

Not many of the islands are large enough for real agriculture. On some a few limes, chillies, pawpaws, pumpkins or watermelons may be grown. A kind of millet used to be widely grown, but most people now prefer to eat imported rice. Some islands grow small but very tasty bananas. The only really important crop is the coconut, which can produce juice, flesh for eating, cooking-oil, fibre for making ropes, and wood for building boats.

There are relatively few birds or animals in Maldives—some reef herons and other sea birds; cats, small rodents but no dogs. A few chickens are kept, and, on some islands, goats. There is not the profusion of insect life found in most tropical countries. In the Maldive Islands there seem to be just enough to feed a few geckos—small lizard-like reptiles that wait for flies on the walls

A cluster of ripening bananas—the Maldives variety is small but full of flavour

of houses, or the long-tailed chameleons which live outside on the trees.

But if there is little striking about life above the water, the diversity and interest of life in the sea is fantastic. Even from a jetty, beach or boat the curved backs of a school of dolphins might be seen as they move along breaking the surface with their rolling dives. On a calm day the surface may be streaked by a flying fish skimming along in a straight line. Sometimes a fish will leap high in the air to escape another hunting it; or, near the beach, a shoal of little silver bait-fish will flutter on the surface as bigger fish move in to feed. Near a coral reef fantastic shapes can be seen through the clear water forming a garden of coral, with flashes of many colours as the reef fish move around.

Reef herons, one of the small number of sea-birds to be found in the islands

A school of dolphins

For a swimmer in mask and snorkel—and preferably fins in case of unexpected currents—who swims over the reef, this underwater scene becomes even more vivid. There will probably be a school of bannerfish, delicate with black and white stripes and banners like long aerials trailing back behind them. Just as delicate but more brightly coloured are the angel-fish and the black and yellow butterfly-fish. Much larger, and with many colours mottling its green back, is the parrot-fish which attacks the coral. Some snorkellers say that they can hear the crunch of its powerful jaws on the hard coral. The coral itself can be seen to be of many varieties—the smooth mounds of brain coral, the

23

twigs of tree coral, the fantastic shapes of vase or mushroom coral. Some of the live coral may look like smooth, strangely-coloured rock; or, where the larger polyps are feeding, it looks like a mass of tiny flowers, as each polyp in the colony tries to catch its meal of plankton in its small tentacles.

In all this beauty, the swimmer must be careful not to touch the coral. Apart from the danger of damaging the live coral, there is the possibility of a scratch that takes a long time to heal. Coral tentacles have a sting to paralyse their prey, and although the sting is very small it is powerful enough to irritate the human skin.

It is unlikely that a swimmer would want to grab hold of a blue and yellow surgeon-fish, but even if he could he might get a bad cut from the scalpel-like sharp fins in the tail that give it its name. And experienced snorkellers know never to stand on the rocky bottom with bare feet, as they might disturb a venomous fish like the stonefish. This ugly-looking creature hides among the stones it resembles and has powerful spines on its back through which it injects a deadly poison into anything standing on it. More attractive in name and appearance but almost as poisonous are its relatives the lionfish and the turkeyfish.

The snorkeller may see other notorious sea creatures—a huge sting-ray waiting for a meal on the sea-bed, or a moray eel with its gaping jaws in a crevice of the coral. In deeper water there might just be a reef-shark, but sharks in the Maldives do not have an evil reputation. In fact, there is so much food in the sea that predators like the sharks do not usually bother with humans at

A diver feeding a moray eel — one of the reef's many predatory fish

all. There is nothing commonly found in the sea round the Maldives which is aggressive unless it is attacked. The real danger is that the human race might cause the extinction of some marine life, killing sea-turtles, for example, to make jewellery from their shells.

Marine life varies according to the environment. Some small fish keep to the sandy shallows of the lagoon, while the most colourful are to be found along the edge of the reef. Other fish again live where the reef slopes down to the sea-bottom. Out in the open sea live the bonito and bluejack tuna that form the staple of the Maldivian economy.

Night-diving has become a popular sport with visitors to Maldives, because it is at night that plankton on the sea-bed rises to the surface; most of the coral opens out to feed and many fish that lie hidden during the day come out to feed as well.

The sea is doubly important to Maldivians today; it provides the fish on which they still depend for food and which earns them foreign currency; and it attracts the tourists who also bring in much of the foreign earnings the country needs for its development. The sea is very special for a country whose land is itself a product of life in the sea.

The Island Nation

The early history of the Maldive Islands is something of a mystery. Since the conversion of the Maldivian people to Islam in the twelfth century, their writers have not generally been interested in anything that happened before then. Recently, however, there has been more interest in the early peoples of the islands, and the origins of the present Maldivians.

It is generally agreed that the Maldivians are related to the Sinhalese of Sri Lanka, and that at one time, like them, they were Buddhist. The Maldivian language, Dhivehi, resembles the Sinhalese language, and both were probably the same about fifteen hundred years ago. But it is not known whether or not the Maldives were settled from Sri Lanka (Ceylon, as it used to be called). The Sinhalese themselves probably migrated from the north-west of the Indian subcontinent; perhaps, at about that time, some of them came to the Maldives instead of to Ceylon.

Because Dhivehi, the island language, is related to the old languages of north-west India, it is part of the family of

27

A five-faced demon, dating back to pre-Islamic times

languages known as Indo-European, to which most modern European languages belong. It is interesting that Maldives is the furthest to the south-east any of these languages spread in ancient times.

On some of the islands there are remains of Buddhist temples; indeed some of the oldest mosques used for prayer by the Maldivians today were probably once Buddhist temples, changed into mosques after the conversion to Islam. On an

28

expedition to the southern atolls in 1985 to look for ancient remains, the Norwegian archaeologist Thor Heyerdal found signs of a considerable Buddhist civilization; it also seems that there may have been Hindu settlement or influence at one time, perhaps from Sri Lanka or southern India. On some of the islands near the Equator, Heyerdal found stone carvings that seem to be of the sun, and he suggested that thousands of years ago, sun-worshipping seafarers might have sailed round the Equator and stopped at or settled in these islands.

The Maldive Islands were certainly well known in early times as a source of cowrie shells. These tiny seashells were used as

A stone carving of the head of the Buddha. It is generally assumed that the population of the islands was once Buddhist

The lavishly decorated interior of one of Malé's ancient mosques. Islam was brought to the islands in the twelfth century

money in many of the lands around the Indian Ocean; gathering and exporting cowries must have been an important part of the economy of the islands before the use of modern currencies.

The islands were also an important source of fresh water and provisions for ships crossing the Indian Ocean. In the twelfth century the sea routes across the Indian Ocean from Arabia and Africa to Malaysia and Indonesia were controlled by the Arabs, whose position in the world had dramatically increased with the expansion of their religion, Islam. Arabs, and other Muslims (followers of Islam), travelled widely to increase their trade and establish their religion. So Muslim scholars as well as merchants travelled along these trade routes.

One of these Muslim scholars, called Abu al-Barakat, perhaps originally Persian, set out from Morocco, in the west of the Muslim world, on a voyage which brought him to Malé, then the capital of the King of Maldives. He is credited with having converted the king and his people to Islam; his tomb in Malé is the holiest place in the nation. The king adopted an Islamic name, Muhammad al Adil, and the Islamic title "Sultan". Maldivian sultans ruled in Malé until 1968; and all Maldivians today still have at least one Islamic name.

Almost two hundred years later another Arab traveller visited Maldives; he was called Ibn Batuta and the books he wrote about his travels are one of our main sources of knowledge about the world at that time. He spent three years in Maldives, and his description of the islands is fascinating. One thing he wrote down was what he was told about the conversion of the Maldivians to Islam. With minor variations this story is still current today. It goes like this: When Abu al-Barakat arrived in Malé he lodged with a family that included a young girl. One day he heard great lamentations in the family and was told that the girl had been chosen as the monthly sacrifice to a sea monster. Every month this monstrous devil came out of the sea and would only be appeased if a virgin was given to him. So every month a girl was chosen to be left in a temple by the sea as an offering to this devil.

The saint offered to take the girl's place; and spent the night reading the Quran, the Muslim holy book containing the word of God revealed to the prophet Muhammad. When the monster appeared, it heard the saint saying the holy words, and it disappeared, never to return.

When the king was told that the saint was still alive in the morning, he vowed to become a Muslim if the monster did not reappear the next month. It did not appear again, and so he and his people obeyed the saint's teachings and became followers of Islam.

Whether or not the conversion was as dramatic and

Maldivians preparing a barbecue. For centuries the islands have been a source of fresh water and provisions for passing ships

The tall minaret of Malé's main mosque

miraculous as in this story, by the time of Ibn Batuta's visit all the people were devout Muslims. They welcomed Islamic scholars and made Ibn Batuta a Cadi, or judge. The island he describes is not very different from Maldivian islands today, with shady streets of coral sand kept swept clean, neat houses and mosques.

The administration of the sultan's government survived with little change until recently, and even the present republican constitution continues many of the same traditions. The tomb of al-Barakat, near the old mosque and the presidential residence

33

in Malé, is kept spick and span with fresh paint, and on holidays it is decorated with flags.

Although Maldives had been Muslim for two hundred years when Ibn Batuta visited, there were still features of Maldivian society which seem to have survived from pre-Islamic times. There were reports of powerful Maldivian queens before Islam, and afterwards there were several female rulers, or sultanas. This was very unusual in an Islamic society. It was a sultana, Khadija, who was on the throne when Ibn Batuta arrived. She was later deposed by her husband, but she murdered him and took the throne again. She then ruled for ten years, at the end of which history repeated itself. She murdered the second husband to depose her, and ruled again for three years before being succeeded by her sister.

One Maldivian custom shocked Ibn Batuta because it was against Muslim ways. This was the women's dress, which was wrapped around the waist leaving the top of the body bare. Eventually, the island women did conform to Mulsim custom, however; a top dress with a beautifully decorated collar became traditional and can still be seen today. However, unlike in most Islamic societies, Maldivian women have never been accustomed to veil their faces.

Although the Maldivians welcomed such visitors from the Islamic world, they were proud of their independence from their stronger neighbours such as India and Ceylon. And the Islamic religion became both a way of keeping Maldivian society together and of marking its separate identity.

A Maldivian girl in the traditional embroidered smock known as the *dhivehi libas*

For centuries the islands came under the influence of Muslim merchant kings from mainland India, called the Ali Rajas. But the only real attempt to conquer the Maldive Islands came in the sixteenth century when Portuguese sailors replaced the Arabs as the dominant power in the Indian Ocean. At that time, the Portuguese led the way in the European race to establish trade with the rich countries of the east. They had been the first to find the way round the south of Africa into the Indian Ocean.

The Portuguese were always ready to take advantage of

internal power struggles to establish themselves in places where they could expand their trade and perhaps gain some converts to Christianity. At the beginning of the sixteenth century they managed to set up a fort and a trading-station in Malé. Then, in 1552, the young Sultan, Hassan IX, who was in the Portuguese colony of Goa in India, became a Christian and granted the Portuguese control of the islands. He seems to have continued to live abroad while his Portuguese masters struggled to consolidate their rule and establish Christianity in the Maldives.

The man regarded as the liberator of the country is Muhammad Thakurufanu. He was the chief of Utheemu, an island in the north. In 1573 he led a small band of Maldivians in an attack on Malé. The members of the Portuguese garrison were killed or driven out; and, despite several attempts to re-establish themselves, they never managed to regain control of the islands.

Today, the anniversary of Thakurufanu's attack, 17 December, is celebrated as National Day, with a special ceremony on his island, Utheemu. The struggle for independence cemented the nation, and reinforced the Maldivian sense of identity based on their Islamic religion. From then on, all Maldivian citizens have had to be Muslim; no foreigner may marry a Maldivian girl or become a citizen without becoming a Muslim.

Although Islam is so important as a social force, it is not interpreted fanatically. Maldivian society has perhaps become more like other Islamic societies than in Ibn Batuta's time, but in many ways the old style of island life has not changed.

36

A military parade to mark the anniversary of the country's battle for independence, celebrated each year on National Day

An interesting example of how the Maldivians adapted to outside influence and their own needs is in their system of writing. Up to the sixteenth century they had used an alphabet, written from left to right, similar to that used by the Sinhalese in Ceylon; now they felt they needed a way of writing where it would be easier to include names and quotation from Arabic, the language of the Quran, which reads from right to left. Some non-Arabic Islamic countries just adopted Arabic writing for their languages, but an unknown Maldivian invented a completely new alphabet for Dhivehi. Like Arabic, it goes from right to left and it uses some Arabic numbers and signs, but it is so well suited to writing down the spoken language that almost

37

Two Maldivian girls. No foreigner may marry a Maldivian woman or become a citizen without first converting to Islam

all Maldivians since then have been able to read and write it easily.

Despite their experience with the Portuguese, the islanders continued to trade with foreigners. When the Dutch (in the seventeenth century) and then the British (in the eighteenth) succeeded the Portuguese as the main powers in the Indian Ocean, the Maldivian sultans made treaties with their governors in Ceylon, and regular trade links were set up.

By the second half of the nineteenth century the Maldivians

had let most of their trade pass into the hands of Indian merchants. A dispute broke out and, in 1887, the sultan signed an agreement with the British to protect his territory from outside interference. Maldives became a British protectorate, but the sultan's government kept complete control of the internal affairs of the country. As there was not even a British representative resident in the islands, Maldives can with some truth claim to be one of the few small countries in the world to have kept it independence during the colonial era. In 1965, the British gave up their protectorate, and Maldives became an independent member of the United Nations.

Although few of the sultans in their capital, Malé, had quite as dramatic reigns as Sultana Khadija in the fourteenth century, political life in the Maldives seems to have been one of the

The ornate underside of the royal umbrella, once used to shade the sultan from the hot sun during ceremonial processions

Wooden shoes on stilts, once worn by the Maldivian rulers. Wearing shoes and carrying umbrellas were royal privileges

constant intrigue. Nevertheless, the sultan and his government (drawn from the leading families of Malé) kept strict control over the life of everyone throughout the islands. The old sultans had some rather strange privileges. For example, only they were allowed to wear shoes or carry umbrellas. They also had a bodyguard which performed a kind of ceremonial fighting on special occasions.

As the twentieth century went on, however, the forms of government changed to seem more in line with current ideas of democracy. In 1932 a *Majlis* or parliament was set up. This was composed partly of elected members, partly of appointed members. A revised constitution was introduced ten years later. As the sultan was old and retired abroad, the prime minister,

40

Muhammad Amin Didi, had control. He started a widespread modernization programme. In 1953, he abolished the sultanate and was declared first President of the Republic of Maldives. The new republic was short-lived. As a fanatical non-smoker, President Didi banned tobacco. This added to financial difficulties, was too much for the people. Within a year the president was out of office and the sultanate re-established.

Then, again in 1968, another powerful prime minister, Ibrahim Nasir, had a new republic declared, and he was appointed president.

Meanwhile, the government in Malé had been faced with trouble in the southern atolls. During the Second World War (1939–45) the British had built two airstrips in the islands as part of their defence of the Indian Ocean. In 1956, they sought Maldivian permission to expand their strip on Gan, an island in Addu, the southernmost atoll, into a major airbase. The islanders in the south had been feeling neglected by the Malé government; in 1959, thinking that they might now get British support, they declared their independence from Malé. Ibrahim Nasir soon came to an agreement with the British, and regained control of the south. Before they left the base at Gan in 1976, the British brought the first taste of modern life to the islands. By then, President Ibrahim Nasir had decided to bring the rest of the country right into the twentieth century, introducing secondary education in English for the people of Malé, building an airport on Hulule island near the capital, and opening the first tourist resorts.

Tourists enjoying windsurfing. In recent years the tourist industry has expanded greatly

President Nasir ruled for ten years, and was replaced by Maumoon Abdul Gayoom, who has carried on opening up relations with the outside world. President Gayoom has brought Maldives into such organizations as the Commonwealth and the South Asian Regional Council. With the help of the United Nations and other aid programmes, he has started widespread development throughout the islands. The most significant change that has taken place is the huge growth of the tourist industry, from one thousand visitors in 1972 to almost 115 thousand in 1986.

In some respects modernization has been very rapid. For many Maldivians completely new opportunities are becoming available. In other ways the traditional life goes on. Reconciling the two will be a challenging task for the Maldivian people.

Island Life, Old and New

The twenty-six natural atolls that form the Maldives are divided into nineteen administrative areas that are also called "atolls". These admininstrative atolls are known by the letters of the Dhivehi alphabet. So the giant Huvadu atoll is divided in two, Gaaf Alif and Gaaf Dhaal ("G/A" and "G/D"), while Addu in the far south is officially known as Seenu ("S"). Malé, the capital, is a separate area, but the natural atoll where it is situated, usually called North Malé atoll, is part of Kaafu ("K") Atoll. Kaafu Atoll also includes the natural atoll south of Malé, and (to the north) the island of Gaafaru on its own reef, and the isolated island called Kaashidhoo. The large irregular group of islands that stretches for about 114 kilometres (90 miles) in the north of Maldives is divided into four, while the island of Fuamulak isolated in the Equatorial Channel is one administrative atoll.

The government controls these far-flung islands as it has always done. It appoints an atoll chief to administer each atoll, and an island chief to be in charge of each inhabited island or

44

A view of an island in one of the twenty-six atolls of the Maldives

village. Dhivehi has the same word for island and village, and each inhabited island does in fact form one community. Only one or two of the largest islands contain more than one village. On one island with two villages there was so much rivalry between them that they had to be separated by a ditch.

The atoll and island chiefs have to keep close watch on what happens in their areas. They have to know who comes to and leaves their islands—foreigners may not land there without permission. They have to report any misconduct, as well as register births, marriages and deaths, and keep an eye of any local development programmes.

Only twenty-five of these islands have populations of over one thousand, so most Maldivians still live in the traditional way as part of a small island community. In these islands the economy is

45

A workman adding finishing touches to a traditional fishing-boat. The country's economy is based on fishing and tourism

usually based on fishing. A typical inhabited island has only a few hundred inhabitants; most families will have lived there for generations, as each family is given land for a house in their island, and it is very difficult to move to another island and get land there. The houses were traditionally built with wood frames, and with walls made of palm leaves and a thatched roof. Many houses are now built of coral blocks with a corrugated -iron roof. All the villagers build walls round their house and garden. Their houses are nearly always arranged along straight, wide streets of coral sand. Just as in Ibn Batuta's time, each household has to keep the street outside its house swept clean.

Apart from each family's house and garden, and the beach for the boats, on every island there is at least one mosque, the island office which is the centre of administration, and probably a school and a football pitch. The rest of the island is used for growing coconuts or, very occasionally, for cultivating vegetables. All land in fact belongs to the government, but some trees and vegetable plots may have been allocated to individuals, while others may belong to the village as a whole. The inhabitants of some islands have the right to gather coconuts or firewood on a nearby uninhabited island, and sometimes an uninhabited island may be leased to an important and favoured individual. He can then make a good profit from its produce.

This favoured individual may also be the island chief; on a

A firewood market in Malé. The wood is gathered on the uninhabited islands—sometimes such islands are leased to individuals

small island the same man may be responsible for seeing that prayers are carried out in the mosque, and for the running of the island school.

Many of the men spend the day at sea; others stay to tend the coconut palms or do various jobs connected with the maintenance and administration of the village. In some islands the craftsmen keep up traditional crafts such as making wooden pots decorated with different coloured layers of laquer; the top layer is scraped off to reveal the colour underneath, forming a fine and intricate design. Most islands have carpenters and builders; islands which used to have silversmiths are now beginning to make coral jewellery to sell to tourists. Other islands specialize in boat-building; and on most beaches, there

Maldivian laquerware, famous for its intricate designs and fine colours

Thatched huts, such as these, serve as boathouses where boats—essential to island life—can be built, kept and repaired

are thatched sheds where the boats are repaired or built in the traditional way, by hand.

The women spend the day preparing food, washing, and keeping the island as neat and tidy as tradition requires. Preparing the food takes up most of the day as many tasks such as sorting and washing the rice and grinding and preparing spices are very time-consuming. The traditional kitchen is a dark and smoky hut of reeds or palm fronds, and most women do as much of their work as possible out of doors. The women are busy in other ways, too—making the family clothes for example. They also often specialize in crafts, such as weaving mats from reeds or screw-pine leaves.

The boats that the men go fishing in have not changed over the

49

An island girl weaving a traditional reed mat

centuries. In fact, they look surprisingly like the boats in old pictures of Viking or Mediterranean galleys with a high curved prow at the front. Until quite recently they had the same square sail, but that has now been replaced by the more efficient triangular sail. Today, most boats also have a diesel engine, but keep the sail for emergency use or for times when the wind is favourable.

The boats, which are typically about twelve metres (forty feet) long, are built principally from coconut wood. Coconut palms in Maldives are unusual in producing good wood for boat building. The trunks of many island palms grow curved because of being exposed to the wind, and these are prized by boat-

50

builders because they fit the curve of the hull. The planks of timber are carved to a fine fit and the seams sealed with coconut fibre. In the old days the planks were fastened together with hard wooden pegs, and Maldivians took pride in having boats with no iron in them. The boats are steered by a long tiller—the helmsman stands on a wide platform at the stern from where the fishing is done. He often uses his foot on the tiller to keep the boat on course.

The men prepare for fishing by netting shoals of little silvery bait-fish; if they can catch the bait close to shore the day before, these are kept in the lagoon in a net or a floating box. When it is time for the boats to set off early in the morning, the bait is put

A pair of fishing-boats. The sails are now only used when the wind is very favourable (or in an emergency). Most of the boats in Maldives today are equipped with diesel engines

Angling for tuna off the coast of Malé

live into the bottom of the boat which is kept flooded with water. The boats set out in search of the tuna. When they find where the tuna is, they close in round the shoal and prepare to fish. One of the men gathers up baskets of bait, and throws the little fish, scattering them around the sea. Other men flail the surface of the sea with paddles. This seems to drive the tuna into a frenzy, making them believe that the sea is alive with tasty morsels. Meanwhile, the fishermen stand on the broad platform at the stern of the boat beside the tiller; their rods and lines have no bait, only silvery hooks that the excited tuna swallow whole, apparently mistaking them for fish. When a fisherman hooks a tuna, he swings it aboard into the hold, where another man takes it off the hook. Then the fisherman swings out his line again.

Although fishing is hard and sometimes dangerous work, and the mainstay of the economy, the fishermen may not make a good living. A large proportion of the day's catch goes to the owner of the boat, and then expenses such as fuel have to be paid for before the remainder of the catch is divided among the six or seven crew members.

If the boats bring back a good catch, the women preserve the fish that will not be eaten that day by drying and smoking it, or boiling it down to make a kind of fish paste. The dried fish is a traditional export—in Sri Lanka, "Maldives fish" is a great

A fish-canning factory, recently opened in Laviyani Atoll

delicacy. The fish paste is used for flavouring, especially when no fresh fish is available.

Most Maldivian meals are basically the same—rice with a curry sauce and tuna, when fish is available, otherwise flavoured with fish paste or flakes of dried fish. Apart from coconut and the hot peppers in the curry, very few vegetables are eaten. One variation in the diet is *roshi*—a kind of pancake baked dry on hot metal and often eaten for breakfast. This diet may not seem very well balanced, but, in fact, many Maldivians seem to thrive on it, with clear skin and eyes, and regular white teeth. The traditional way to clean the teeth, by the way, is with sand and water. However, most of the food value in the diet is from fish, and if

Girls sorting rice, a traditional staple food in Maldives

An old Maldivian woman smoking a water-pipe

there is stormy weather and catches are bad, poor families may suffer from quite severe malnutrition.

On Fridays the women help the men haul the boats onto the beach to clean and repair them; this is a major social event, for there is little to break the slow pace of island life. Most of the time when people are not working is spent sitting on a swing or a rope chair (called a *joli*) under a tree in the yard, chatting, smoking (the older women prefer water-pipes), or just sitting. The boys play football, or some other ball game, and the girls often play a kind of tennis called *bashi*, where one girl serves with her back to the net and those on the other side try to catch the ball. As only the largest islands have any traffic at all, the children are able to play quite freely in the streets. Although the island children do not have organized games or manufactured toys, they can make their own toy boats, or whistles from coconut leaves. And, of course, they can all swim.

Daily life is regulated by the calls to prayer from the mosque. Following the instructions of the Prophet Muhammad, the founder of Islam, Muslims should pray five times a day, summoned by a call from the mosque. The first call comes at the first light of dawn, but before praying a Muslim must wash himself thoroughly. For a Maldivian islander this means going to the fenced-off part of the garden containing the well. He draws up water in a scoop fastened to the end of a long stick. He then empties the scoop over himself, and repeats the process a number of times. Most Maldivians will say their morning prayer in their house, but the men, if not at sea, will try to go to the mosque for the mid-day prayer, especially on Friday. Friday is the Muslim day of rest, but before mid-day prayers many of the men will be busy cleaning the boats. Women generally pray at home, except when a part of the mosque is set aside for them. Some islands have a special women's mosque. Then there are three other prayer calls—half-way through the afternoon, at sunset and when it is completely dark.

Children on most islands have always had some kind of an education, going to classes either at the mosque or at a little privately-run school, or being taught at home. They learn to read and write Dhivehi, do simple arithmetic, and, most

Island women swaying rhythmically as they tap metal pots with the rings on their fingers to accompany the traditional dance

important, to recognize Arabic script and to say the Arabic prayers. Although modern education has only come recently to Maldives, almost every Maldivian can read and write Dhivehi a little.

There is not much in the way of evening entertainment; lighting is poor and expensive—usually by oil-lamp, sometimes by electricity from a small generator. Most people go to bed early. On special occasions there may be a dance: the *bodu beru* (big drum) for the men can get quite frenzied, and an extreme version of it which ends with the dancers stabbing their heads with knives had to be prohibited by the government. The women have a gentler, swaying dance, done as they tap metal pots with the rings on their fingers. One of the special occasions may be a

57

circumcision ceremony. The operation is performed on boys when they are about seven years old; for several days afterwards, while they are recovering, they lie in bed. Whenever they are awake, they are entertained by their family and friends.

The year is broken up by Muslim feasts and fasting. The Arabs use a lunar calendar, that is one where each month begins at the new moon—this makes the year approximately ten days shorter than the Western calendar year. During the month of Ramadan, Muslims fast. They do not eat, drink or smoke between dawn and sunset. When they hear the sunset prayer call, Maldivians

Selling coconut-juice. This refreshing drink is dispensed for each customer direct from the coconut shell

may break their fast with a drink of coconut juice before going to the mosque. The rest of the evening is taken up with eating and visiting friends. During the night the women have to prepare a meal to be eaten before the first light of dawn. As might be expected, not much other work gets done during the day in Ramadan. The end of the fasting month is celebrated as the Kuda Eid—the Little Holiday. The Bodu Eid—the Big Holiday—is during the *haj*, or pilgrimage, when the well-off go on their once-in-a-lifetime journey to the Muslim holy places in Saudi Arabia. It may be celebrated by the sacrifice of a goat if there is one, but most Maldivians make a special rice curry with fish or if possible chicken, which they share with friends and neighbours.

As well as the Muslim calendar and now the Western calendar, Maldivians have their own system of dividing up the year, based on the weather and on fishing conditions. The year is divided into twenty-seven periods of thirteen or fourteen days. For example, the period from February 1 to 13, when the weather is dry and the fishing good, is called Dinasha; April 8 to 21 is hot and dry with poor fishing—this is the time for planting; in Funors, June 3 to 16, bad weather is expected, so no islander will plan a journey for then.

Perhaps the strangest thing about traditional island life is the rate of marriage and divorce. Most people get married early; and it is considered quite usual for husband or wife to want to divorce and marry someone else. About eighty per cent of marriages end in divorce, and most older people have been

59

A Maldivian girl at work. When she marries it will be according to the Muslim tradition but many such marriages end in divorce

married several times. An old person might well have been married and divorced ten times, perhaps several times to and from the same person! It is quite common for family rows to end in divorce but for the couple to come back together again later. Divorce is easy, particularly for the man, who can just tell his wife he is divorcing her. And marriage, because it is not likely to be long-lasting, is not celebrated with much ceremony. Moreover, Islamic law allows a man to have up to four wives at one time, as long as he can treat them equally; but having two wives at a time is not common in Maldives, and more than two very rare.

60

Although the islands are remote and lacking in modern facilities, the people do have help with the difficult things in life. Many people are skilled in traditional ways of helping the sick, and some women specialize in looking after others when they are giving birth. Belief in spirits, or *jinn*, is common—many of these ideas date from before the conversion to Islam. On most islands there is a man who is an expert in *fandita*—a blend of traditional skills, superstition and religion. The *fandita* man will perform ceremonies to cure the sick, help the fishing, make a newly-planted tree flourish, or even bring about a desired marriage. Many islanders would rather entrust themselves to a *fandita* man when sick than risk an uncomfortable voyage of several days to the hospital in Malé. Even in Malé, many people still trust the *fandita* man—for example, to find stolen possessions when the police are baffled. For life in Malé today has changed considerably from the traditional ways, and theft, previously virtually unknown, is an occasional problem.

Life in Malé

The capital is now very crowded, with almost sixty thousand people in its 2.6 square kilometres (one square mile), and the emphasis is on education and contact with the outside world. Most of the population are there for education, or are connected with government, with trade, or in some way with the tourist industry. Because it is the capital and the place where the population is concentrated, it has facilities hardly dreamed of in some islands. Malé people with a choice of well trained doctors as well as the Central Hospital do not really need the *fandita* man.

Malé houses are mostly built of coral or cement blocks, set behind high coral walls. Modern concrete houses are being built of two or more storeys, and a few four or five-storey office blocks and shopping centres are also going up. Every house is crowded—a small three-room house may have fifteen occupants—and the streets are full of activity, especially when the schools are coming out. But the main centre of activity in Malé is the waterfront; one section is busy with tourist boats and boats for

62

Schoolchildren playing in an island street

the airport, another with bigger boats from distant islands, while in another barges unload freight from the ships anchored offshore. Probably the busiest place is in front of the fish market, where the day's catch is unloaded. Here, islanders load up with all the things their island needs—because all goods have to be bought in Malé. Beside the fish market are a firewood market, a little fruit and vegetable market, and a warren of shops selling everything under the sun.

Many kinds of boats and shipping can be seen from the waterfront. Most are the traditional fishing-boat or *dhoni*. If they have come from a distant island they may have a coconut-thatch shelter for the crew and passengers—for there is no regular

63

Boats with coconut-thatch shelters for the crew and passengers to protect them during their voyage from a distant island

transport between the islands, and most passengers have to squeeze into whatever boat is going. As dark falls a spark glows from each boat as the crew light a small oil-stove to cook supper.

Tourist *dhonis* are decked. They have wooden seats and a canopy to keep off the sun and rain. These may be slightly more comfortable than the old *dhonis*, but tourists have to be hardy to face a long voyage if the weather is bad—some resorts are several hours away from the airport—and a few modern launches are now to be seen. Some larger *dhonis* have been fitted with cabins for visitors who would like to cruise round the islands, and there are now modern cruising yachts to be seen as well. Sometimes a large trading *dhoni* comes in to Malé with its two or three sails set,

64

but most cargo is carried in an ungainly motorized version piled high with goods of all kinds.

Outside the harbour are anchored the sea-going ships, some old and rusty, some smart and modern, carrying on a brisk trade with Colombo (in Sri Lanka) or Singapore. These unload into barges that are towed by tugs to a new Customs berth. The tugs have another use, too, for every so often an unwary captain misses his channel and puts his ship on a reef. He can then only hope that there will soon be a high tide and that the tugs will be powerful enough to pull him off.

A souvenir shop in Malé

Behind the waterfront are government offices and new shops to attract the tourists to buy souvenirs. And, in what used to be the middle of the town there are the old mosque, the tomb of al-Barakat, and the President's Palace, surrounded by a few old houses belonging to the former nobility. This only used to be the centre, because the town has expanded to cover the whole island, and further—the lagoon on the south side has been filled in to provide more land for building. The island has doubled in size in ten years, as well as trebling in population.

Formerly in Malé, as on the other islands, the streets were of shining coral sand, with practically no vehicles. When it rained, the water drained away through the sand, leaving a dry firm surface. As Malé expanded, more and more people took to cycling to and from work or the market, and now there are more

A view of a street in Laamu Atoll. It is made of pure coral sand, ideal for pedestrians and cyclists but unsuited to motor vehicles

Bicycles outside the municipal hospital in Malé. There are over six thousand registered bicycles in the capital

than six thousand bicycles registered in Malé. Luggage and goods used to be carried in two-wheeled hand-carts; these are now being replaced by small pick-ups. A few taxis have also been introduced. With more construction work and trading, trucks are coming into use, and a few rich people have private vehicles, although they can seldom get out of first or second gear, and the longest road is only 1.6 kilometres (one mile) long. When it rains, this new traffic digs holes in the sand and compacts it so that the water cannot drain away. Huge puddles are formed in the roads. Some roads are flooded right across their width and getting around town is a problem. Some people wade through the water wearing rubber sandals, others cycle through, lifting their feet

Sewage pipes now being installed in Malé

above the water when it gets too deep, and hoping their wheels will not go into a deep hole or a patch of soft mud. As the roads get worse, more people take to taxis. But the taxis, too, have difficulty getting through—and the road conditions worsen. Now the government is putting a concrete surface on the main roads and major drainage, sewage and water schemes are under way.

Traditionally, Maldivians have taken the water they need for drinking, cooking and washing from wells dug in the garden. Although the coral forming the islands is soaked through with seawater, the fresh rainwater sinking through the sand forms

68

what is called a "lens", floating on top of the denser saltwater. If the well is just the right depth, it will fill with good fresh water. Some islands have better water than others—that is the main reason why so few are inhabited. The population explosion in Malé has been too much for the ground supply of fresh water, which has also been contaminated by the lack of proper sewage facilities. So now, in Malé, well water can only be used for washing. Rainwater for drinking has to be collected off the roofs of the houses and stored in special tanks. Families without rainwater tanks have to collect fresh water from special tanks at the mosques. As the dry weather sets in, longer and longer queues of women and children carrying pots and containers form outside these mosques.

Everyday life in Malé is very busy compared with life in the

Women queuing for drinking water at a communal well

other islands. Government offices work from 7.30 am to 1.30 pm; as salaries are low, most workers have another job in the afternoon or evening. Shops are generally open until 11.00 pm, only closing for half an hour or so at prayer times.

Because of the numbers of schoolchildren, schools work several shifts. In the secondary schools, for example, the senior pupils may come to school from 7.00 am to 1.00 pm and the junior classes from 1.30 to 6.00 pm. Primary schools are even more crowded; the first-year classes, with over five hundred pupils in the first year in a single school, may come for three hours. As they go home, the second year comes in. Later on, it is the turn of the third and the fourth years. The streets near the schools are often closed to traffic as the classes change. The little children are usually brought to school by older members of the family; sometimes they are wheeled along sitting on the saddle of their brother's bicycle. Because the school day is short and crowded, and children have little to keep them busy during the rest of the day, they are often sent to private tutorial classes as well. Many of these children have come from other islands to get an education, and they stay with family friends or relatives, whom they help with housework and with other jobs.

There are not enough Maldivian teachers to cope with the sudden increase in the demand for education; most of the teachers come from Sri Lanka. There are many other workers from Sri Lanka and other countries, working on development and construction projects. This adds to the crowding but, with the foreign visitors, it gives Malé an international air.

Maldivian schoolchildren in their classroom. Many of the island schools suffer from overcrowding and children are taught in shifts

Life in Malé is a mixture of traditional and new. People are awakened by the dawn call to prayer from the mosque, but in Malé it is amplified electronically. Some modern houses may have showers installed, but still the morning wash is time-consuming with people getting ready for prayers, people getting ready for work, and schoolchildren having to be clean and neat in their uniforms for seven o'clock classes.

In the late afternoon, some of the young men not at school or work go to the football match—there is only room for one stadium, so all the teams play there, and during the season there is a match nearly every day. They may listen to the match on the radio, or watch it next day on television. In the evening, Malé people may go to the cinema, or, if they are lucky enough to have

A shady street in Maldives. Most houses have at least one tree to shade the roof from the hot sun

a video, they may hire a popular English or Indian movie. But mostly, in the evening, the people of Malé like to sit and chat with their friends, to wander around the streets, or just to stand at the door of their house. If they do not see any of their friends passing by, they may call them up on the telephone.

So modern ways have modified rather than replaced the old traditions. The old men have local mosques to go to at prayer time, but there is also a magnificent new mosque in the town centre for special occasions. Circumcision ceremonies are celebrated as before, but now they always take place in the school holidays, and include the latest popular music on a stereo system as well as the *bodu beru*.

72

With the houses so close together it is always easy to hear what entertainment is going on in the next house, even if the high walls give some privacy. Although there is not much space for gardens, most houses have enough space alongside them for at least one tree, to shade the roof, and to sit under in a *joli* or swing.

Strangely enough, in a country with so many uninhabited islands, Malé is not the only crowded island. Several islands in the atolls have as great a density of population, with up to ten thousand people crammed into a tiny area.

One feature of island life that survives in crowded Malé is the neatness and orderliness. Indeed, it is probably because of this that life there can go on. At first sight, Malé does not look all that busy or thickly populated. From the air it looks remarkably green, with the trees shading the house roofs. The streets are broad and—for much of the time—quiet. Visitors do not see beggars, or poor people sleeping on the streets. The National Security Service, which combines the roles of police, army and coastguard, makes sure there are no disturbances. They are particularly keen to see that nobody cycles the wrong way up a one-way street, or without a lamp after 6.00 pm, which is about the time that darkness falls throughout the year. There is still comparatively little serious or violent crime in Malé. If someone does something which the government disapproves of, they may be placed under house arrest; that is, made to stay at home. If they are convicted in the courts of a crime, they will probably be banished—the traditional punishment of being sent to live on a distant island for a certain number of months or years.

A man in the traditional *lungi,* or sarong. Younger men often prefer Western shirts and trousers

In some ways Malé people adopt modern ideas from outside. Young Malé couples may celebrate their wedding and trust they can stay together for life. In dress, the government expects its male employees to wear Western shirts and trousers instead of the *lungi* or sarong. For women, a wide collared dress covering wrists and ankles was introduced by the first president, but most girls prefer a long tunic and trousers for the office and a Western-style skirt and blouse at home. The old *dhivehi libas* with

74

its embroidered neckline is worn by older women and on special occasions.

Girls in Malé have an equal chance of education with boys, and a few of them get comparatively high positions in the government. But no woman can become president. That is one way in which the Maldives constitution has followed the Islamic tradition rather than the old Maldivian tradition which produced queens like Khadija.

Tourism and Development

Tourism started in Maldives in a small way in 1972, when a few small cabins were built on an island near the new airstrip on Hululu, and one charter plane arrived from Colombo, the capital of Sri Lanka. These first adventurous tourists did not mind the primitive conditions because they had discovered a tropical island paradise, and more and more of the uninhabited islands within easy reach of Hululu were developed into tourist resorts. These were quite simple; a row of cabins facing the beach, a restaurant and a small bar. As more tourists came and more flights came into Hululu from Sri Lanka and India, the airport was developed until it became capable of taking the largest jets. Today, up to three airliners can be accommodated at the airport at once, and regular flights between Europe and the Far East stop there.

As the numbers of tourists have increased more and more new resorts have been opened; now almost every suitable island in North Malé atoll is a resort, and there are more in South Malé atoll. Resorts have been opened in Alif atoll to the east of Malé, and further afield. Meanwhile, some resorts have been modernized, and they rival the luxury hotels of Sri Lanka in comfort.

What is there for a holidaymaker in Maldives? The major attraction is the peace and restfulness. Lying in the sun, or in the shade of a coconut palm, on a bright beach of soft coral sand, beside a clear sea of brilliant blues and emerald greens, is many people's idea of paradise. The weather is pleasantly warm, with a cool breeze from the sea, or a dip in the sea itself to refresh them. Most of the tourists come from Europe and Japan, from countries where cold winters—as well as enough money and time—encourage people to travel to a place in the sun.

For the more energetic there are water-sports available, such as windsurfing—with the warm clear sea and sandy bottom there is no discomfort in falling in. The main sport is of course snorkelling, or (for the more experienced) diving. Almost every tourist island has its diving school. A good instructor is essential for new divers, as diving can be dangerous for the inexperienced, and the currents in the sea can be strong and unpredictable. It is not unknown for divers to go down from a boat and come up later to find they have drifted far away from the boat.

Many tourists make at least one trip to a nearby inhabited island as well as a tour round Malé. These are about the only times that the world of the tourist and the ordinary Maldivian meet, for the Maldivians are not encouraged to visit tourist islands except to work there. In fact, many of the workers in

77

A snorkeller descending towards a coral "garden" on the sea-bed

direct contact with the tourists on these islands are Sri Lankan. This separation of the tourist from the ordinary Maldivian means that the visitors can be allowed to enjoy such un-Islamic things as pork, alcohol, and scanty clothing on their islands.

But, in spite of this separation of tourism from ordinary life, the development of the tourist industry has had a significant effect on the ordinary Maldivian. Young Maldivian men have

78

always been accustomed to leave their islands to work on ocean-going ships, but now far more are going to work in resorts. Their families, left at home, may have more money than they were accustomed to, but they also have less of a role in the community. They have to buy food in from Malé, rather than share in the fishermen's catch, and their diet may not, in fact, be so healthy. The better-off men with boats may also find that they can make more money if they give up fishing and convert their boats to carry tourists or supplies to the islands.

Some islands near resorts have become very dependent on the tourists. The Maldivians there make souvenirs and sell them when visitors come on a trip to see village life. In Malé, too, selling things to tourists has become a thriving business. Even more important is the business of supplying the resorts with

A view of an isolated tourist beach. The Maldivian government has confined tourism to designated islands, to prevent the spread of Western values and lifestyles to the local Muslim population

food and all they need to function — practically everything used on the resorts is imported. This also means that prices in the resorts are quite high, but so are the expenses. As a result, as much of the management and investment in the resorts also comes from abroad, the Maldivian economy does not benefit from the revenue from tourism as much as it otherwise might.

In 1987, the government of Maldives, with help from international agencies, set up a School of Hotel and Catering Services to train Maldivians to take a greater part in their own tourist industry. This is a project which will take a long time to have any real effect; the thirty or so Maldivians trained there in a year have to provide the future trainers and administrators as well as experts in all branches of the tourist business. The time taken to train workers in new skills and technology is a problem for all the many new developments now taking place or planned in Maldives.

Few countries have seen as much change as has Maldives in the past twenty years. Today, with so much contact with the outside world and help being offered from many development agencies, the new ways are taking root and spreading throughout the country. International bodies such as the United Nations, and development programmes from friendly countries or voluntary organizations work with the Maldivian government to improve economic prospects and social conditions.

The economy of Maldives has always been based on fishing, and the fishing industry is being expanded and modernized. A new kind of fishing-boat, called the "second generation *dhoni*" has been developed. In many ways it is similar to the old boats, but it has been designed to use a diesel engine and is much more efficient. The old technique of catching tuna with rod and line and baitless hooks is being retained—for one thing it prevents overfishing ruining the stocks of tuna—but the marketing and processing has changed.

The boats no longer bring the catch home. Instead they deliver it to government-run collector-vessels anchored in the atolls. Most of the catch is sold for freezing for direct export. Over 18,000 tonnes of frozen skipjack tuna are now exported annually. In addition, a modern canning factory has been opened by the government so that Maldives now exports its own brand of tinned tuna. Some Maldives fish is still smoked at home, but the export market is handled by the government-run State Trading Organization as well. Fishermen have also begun catering for the tastes of people in other parts of the world, preparing delicacies such as dried shark's fin for the Singapore market.

About twenty-eight per cent of the labour force works in the fishing industry, but this is only half what it used to be. Fishermen's wages are now much less than those of most other workers. The use of diesel engines in the boats has greatly increased the catches, as boats can now go out further and in varying weather conditions. But the fuel has to be paid for, and the boat-owner needs an extra share to pay back the money he borrowed from the government to buy the engine. So the ordinary members of the crew do not get much benefit, and

A fisherman with a fine tuna catch. Over twenty-eight per cent of the nation's workforce is employed in the fishing industry

young men in the islands may prefer to work on development projects, or go away to get a job in a tourist resort. These new types of work are better paid; but unless the worker can get some training he is unlikely to keep such a job for very long.

One other traditional source of foreign earnings for Maldivians was employment on foreign ships. But this has declined in recent years, and the tourist industry is now the other main source of income. Because of the foreign earnings from fishing and tourism, the Maldivian currency, the *rufiyya*, is quite stable. Prices do not vary much; the price of essential food imports, such as rice and sugar, is kept low by the government; and, so far, most Maldivians are willing to do without other imports which are very highly priced.

Some attempts have been made to set up other industries on different islands. Clothing manufacture is being tried, but the materials have to be imported and so does the labour, for it appears that Maldivians do not like factory life. There might be better prospects for developing local handicrafts, as Maldivians have many unique skills and there is a ready market among the tourists, but this would be unlikely to become a major industry.

Many of these schemes involve islands away from Malé, for it is now government policy to improve the facilities away from the capital. Introducing modern industry, education and social welfare in the remote islands should reduce the numbers of people coming to Malé. This would make it possible for life on Malé to run smoothly, and at the same time give equal opportunities to people living in all parts of the country.

With the population spread out over so many small islands, the first need is for improved communications. Every inhabited island has a radio link with the atoll office, which itself has a link with the capital. Today, the island and atoll chiefs make their reports by radio. An inter-atoll telephone service is being set up, and broadcasting is being established to include programmes that will help the island communities take part in development. International satellite communication by telephone and telex is good. Maldives has had a postal service since 1906, and has always tried to make its stamps attractive to collectors. However, as yet there is no postal service outside Malé.

Transport between the remote islands and Malé has always

been slow and hazardous. Even within an atoll it may be difficult to find a boat to go to another island, and if the destination is on the other side of the atoll, the journey might take up the best part of a day. Modern transport between the islands and the capital is surprisingly difficult to develop. Some high-speed launches and sea-planes have been used, but the treacherous coral reefs just below the surface of the sea present great problems. Modern materials moving at high speed are easily torn apart by a coral reef. Slow solid wooden boats with a shallow draught can nose their way through the reef—if they scrape the coral, no harm is done. The programme to build boats that combine the virtues of the traditional craft with modern technology is therefore vital; another important project is to improve harbour facilities on developing islands so that larger boats can berth there. New jetties are being built, and reefs enclosing harbours are being blasted to make new entrances.

Air transport can also connect the more distant islands if they are big enough for a runway; there is a regular service to Gan in Addu atoll in the south, which stops at a new airport in Laamu atoll. Both these airports are on islands which are part of chains of long islands fringing the atolls, and in both atolls nearby islands have been joined by causeways. Roads have been built so that motor transport can now be used there and industrial development is planned, with new garment, canning and boat-engine factories.

Each atoll has a capital which is the centre of its administration. If there is another large inhabited island in the atoll this may also be selected for special development. In one of these islands in each atoll will be found an Atoll Education Centre which is both the primary school for that island, and a centre for the development of education in the atoll. Islands that do not have a full primary school themselves may send pupils to the Atoll Education Centre. Transport and boarding are problems, but some Atoll Education Centres are now building dormitories. However, the main problem is still finding local people with enough education to train as teachers, for education outside Malé is in the Dhivehi language, and vacancies cannot be filled by foreign teachers. Secondary schools are planned for the atolls, too, so that pupils continue their education without having to go to Malé; but it will be many years before children all over the country have a chance to complete the seven years of primary education, let alone go on to secondary education. Other kinds of training have also been started; on some islands Vocational Training Centres have been set up, to train island youngsters in boat-building and other crafts.

Each atoll has a Health Centre, staffed either by doctors or trained Community Health Workers. There islanders can get an examination and treatment, or can be advised to go to the central hospital in Malé. Several small regional hospitals are also under construction in selected atolls.

Training takes place in Malé for nurses going to work at the central hospital, and for nurses and health workers going to the atolls. There are also centres in Malé for training technicians and craftsmen. Maldives cannot hope to provide university or advanced training. One main reason for having secondary education in English is that Maldivian students can then easily get places in universities abroad. The gap between the English-medium education in Malé and the new primary schools teaching in Dhivehi on the islands should narrow, as the atoll schools develop and the Malé schools concentrate more on Dhivehi subjects. At present, there is a desperate shortage of educated and trained government administrators. This is particularly serious in a country where trade and industry are largely controlled by government organizations.

Malé itself has its own expansion programme. New facilities are planned for the area reclaimed from the lagoon, and there are plans to develop the nearest tourist island, Villingili, as a

An island hospital. Its nursing staff has been trained in the main hospital in Malé, which also trains atoll health workers

residential suburb of Malé, so it is likely that the attraction of the capital will continue.

Development also brings its hazards. One arises from the mining of coral for building from the reefs around the islands. If the protection of these reefs is broken, the islands will be at the mercy of the sea. Already Malé has suffered from the effects of pushing out to its reef. In 1987, during a period of high tides and heavy seas, much of the reclaimed land was flooded. Buildings were damaged and the water-table polluted. A new, very expensive sea-wall will have to be built to replace the protection the reef gave naturally.

The Future of Maldives

In spite of such problems, Maldivians realize the importance of conserving the natural environment. Not only do the main industries of fishing and tourism depend on it, but the land itself is built up by biological processes. The nation has only survived over the centuries because its way of life is in tune with the natural environment. So plans are usually made for new developments to come out of the old ways. New schools on the islands, for example, will grow out of the traditional ones, not replace them. The Ministry of Health brings in the island women experienced in helping with births to learn the latest techniques in health-care and midwifery. Infant mortality (the number of babies that die soon after birth) has been halved in ten years to fifty-eight per thousand births. These new midwives use scientific methods, but combine them with traditional ones, and the mothers are encouraged to relax in the confidence that they are getting the best of the old and the new.

The Republic of Maldives still has a long way to go—in spite of the jumbo jets landing on Hulule—before it is a developed country. The infant mortality rate is still too high, but the birth-rate is also too high. The population growth of 3.7 per cent per year is one of the highest in the world, and the habitable islands could soon become overcrowded. Maldivians now live for an average of fifty-two years, and forty-five per cent of the population is under fifteen. With the government struggling to provide education and social services for the present population, can it continue the development to cope with an ever-growing population? Everywhere there is a shortage not just of trained people, but also people with enough basic education to acquire the skills needed in a modern economy. Added to this, there is a shortage of educated people to train as teachers to provide that basic education. It would be a tragedy if these beautiful islands became overcrowded and unable to support their people at the same time as industry could not develop because of a labour shortage.

There is also a danger that things could change too quickly for the people to adapt to the new way of life. Will a new educated generation accept the constant regulation of their lives by the Malé government? How can traditional beliefs of decent morality survive when the country depends so much on catering for fun-seeking foreigners? How can the old culture survive when schools are teaching so many new ideas from outside?

On the other hand, Maldives has many advantages. It has a stable society, a long history of self-reliance, and no external

A young Maldivian couple bathing their baby. What will the child's future be like in Maldives' rapidly changing-economy and culture?

enemies. The people are intelligent and adaptable. With luck, in the future Maldives will be a real tropical paradise both for the Maldivians and for their visitors.

Index

91

92